*For my sweet Maranatha Melody
and in memory of Nathanael Dorian*

Songs for Little Love Bugs

Illustrated by Cynthia Butler

featuring the songs of Canopy

**Music can be downloaded at
www.canopymusic.net/lovebugs
password: letmein**

Copyright © 2019 by Canopy

ISBN: 978-1-7322815-0-9

Good Morning To You

Birds are singing just outside,

"Good morning to you."

Open up your little eyes.

Good morning to you.

Good morning, good morning.

The sun is brightly shining.

Good morning, little love bug.

Good morning to you!

Let's Get Dressed

Little love bug, let's get dressed.

Let's see that you look your best:

Hat, pants, shirt, vest,

Yes, yes, let's get dressed.

Love Bug

Here's a little love bug; here's another.
They attach to each other.
Then they fly around together.
Everywhere that he goes, she goes too.
They can teach me and you
Love, love, love, whatever you do.

Here's a little bee, and here's another.
They give honey to each other.
Then they eat it all together.
One day Mister Bee said, "Sweet Miss Bee,
Honey, won't you marry me?
Then I'll give you a wedding ring."

Flower Child

When you were a tiny baby you were like a little seed.
And your life had just begun
When God planted you inside of me.
Then you spread your roots within the soil of my womb
'Til the day that you were born;
Then you began to bloom.

My flower child, oh, when you smile,
You are more radiant than all the colors of spring;
The tulips bright, the lilies white;
They're not the reason that the birds begin to sing.
They sing for love in all its gentle power.
And I love you, my little flower child.

There's a Bear In Your Hair

There's a bear, there's a bear,

There's a bear in your hair;

There's a bear in your hair, and it's goin' nowhere.

There's a bear, there's a bear,

There's a bear in your hair;

There's a hair-dwellin' bear in your hair.

Right there!

When You Have a Bath

When you have a bath,

You're kind of slippery.

When you have a bath,

We wash your body.

We wash you here,

We wash you there,

We wash you from your hair

To your little derrière.

Hippopotamus

The hippopotamus: we like him a lotamus,
And we're just madapus about the platypus.
We're all quite aware of the polar bear,
And the elephant is an essential element.
But of all the animals, you're just outstandimal.
I would trade a whole zoo for just one of you.
We're each a fanelope of the antelope,
And the centipede is such a sight to see.
Oh, the octopus is downright cute-opus.
And you are too-topus
from your head to your gluteus maximus.
Yes sir, that's a faximus!

Sleep, Little Caterpillar

Sleep, little caterpillar; rest your head.

I'll wrap you up in a blanket cocoon.

Sleep, little caterpillar, in your bed.

You'll be a butterfly soon.

Now you crawl, and now you squirm;

Cute as a bug and wiggly as a worm.

But some day soon you'll spread your wings

And do some really amazing things.

And I know it's hard to take a break

With such big things to do.

But even the tiniest creatures

Need some shut-eye, too.

Dreams Take Flight

A ship is sailing in your mind,

Carrying you from the shore

Of daylight discoveries

To a magic twilight tour.

The waters rock you gently

As you glide beneath the stars,

Their light reflected on the waves

Like fireflies in jars…

None have sailed this way before.

There is no plotted course.

Steer your boat into moonlight.

Watch your dreams take flight.

Good Morning To You

Words & Music by Cynthia Butler

Birds are sing-ing just out-side, "Good morn-ing to you."

O-pen up your lit-tle eyes. Good morn-ing to you. Good

morn-ing, good morn-ing. The sun is bright-ly shin-ing. Good

morn-ing, lit-tle love bug. Good morn-ing to you!

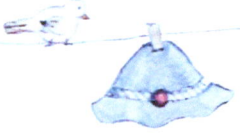
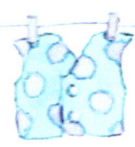

Let's Get Dressed

Words & Music by Cynthia Butler

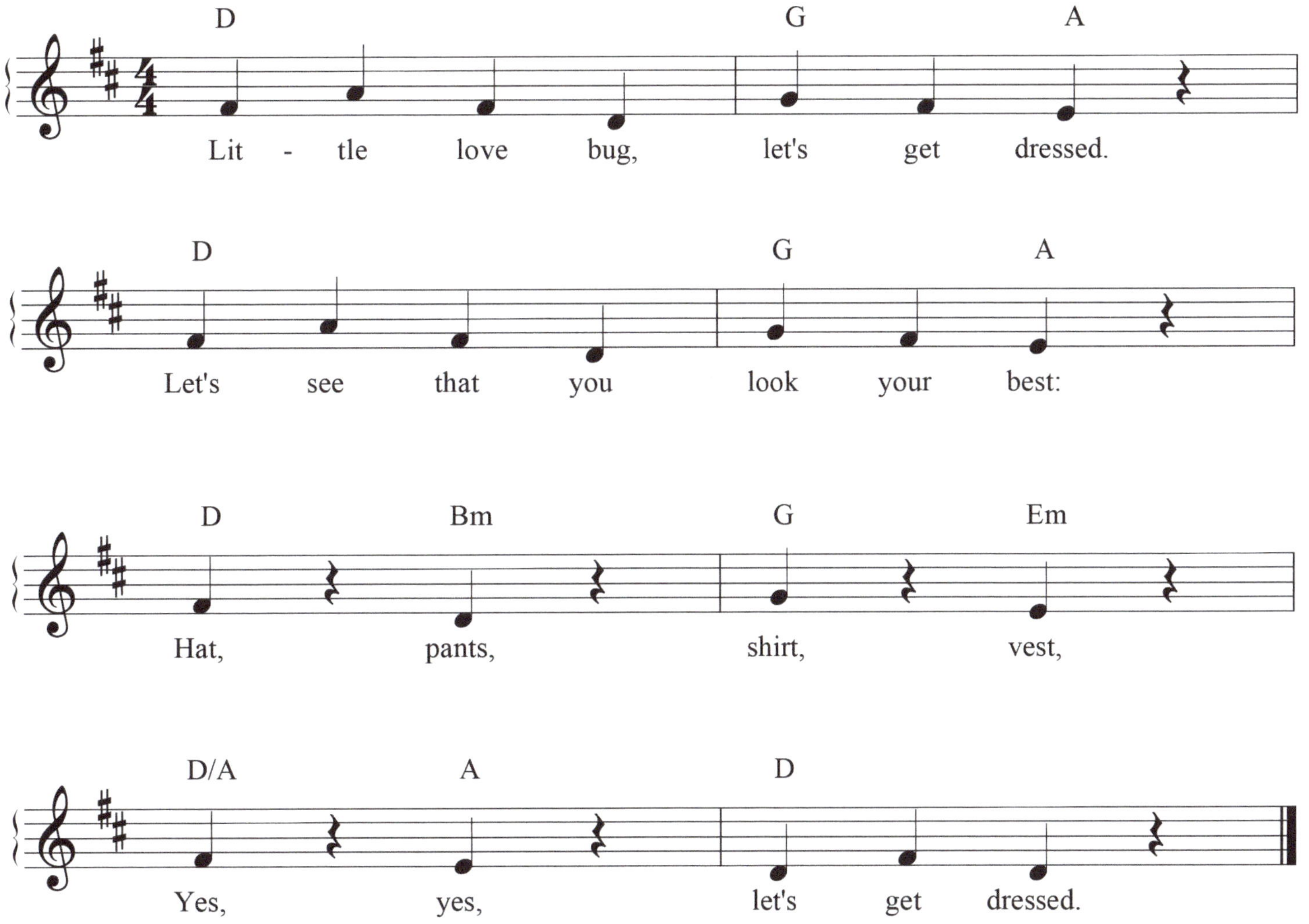
D G A
Lit - tle love bug, let's get dressed.
D G A
Let's see that you look your best:
D Bm G Em
Hat, pants, shirt, vest,
D/A A D
Yes, yes, let's get dressed.

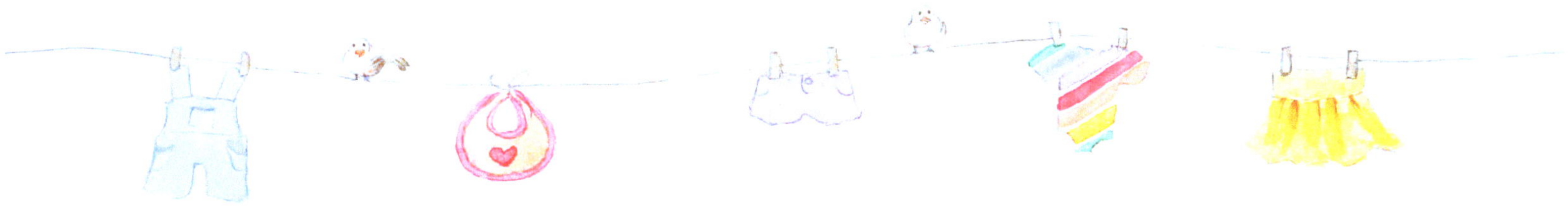

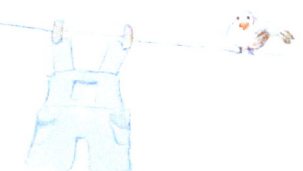

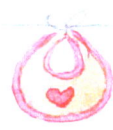

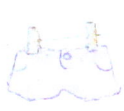

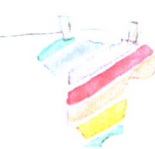

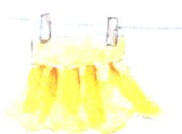

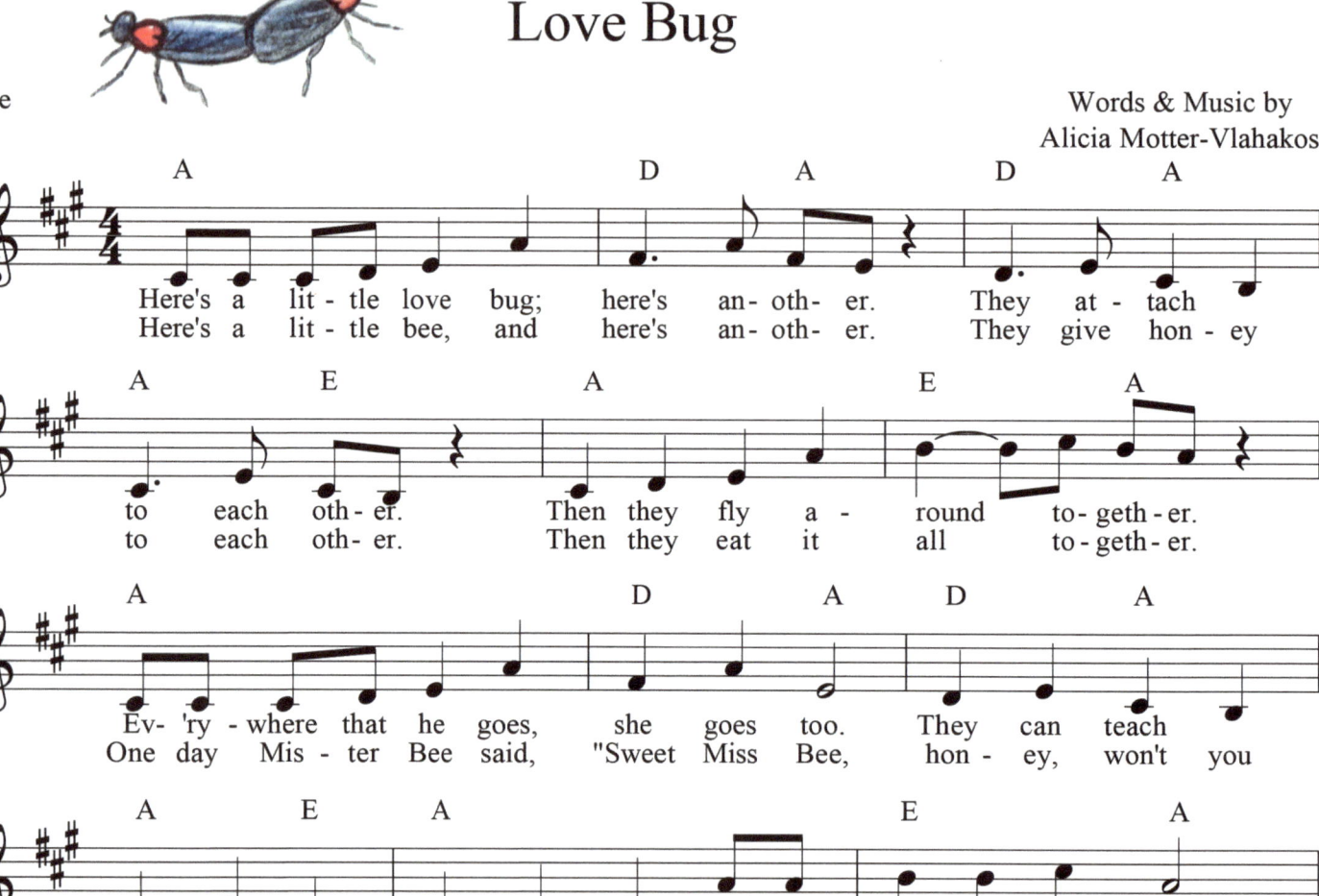

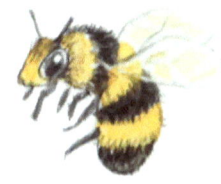

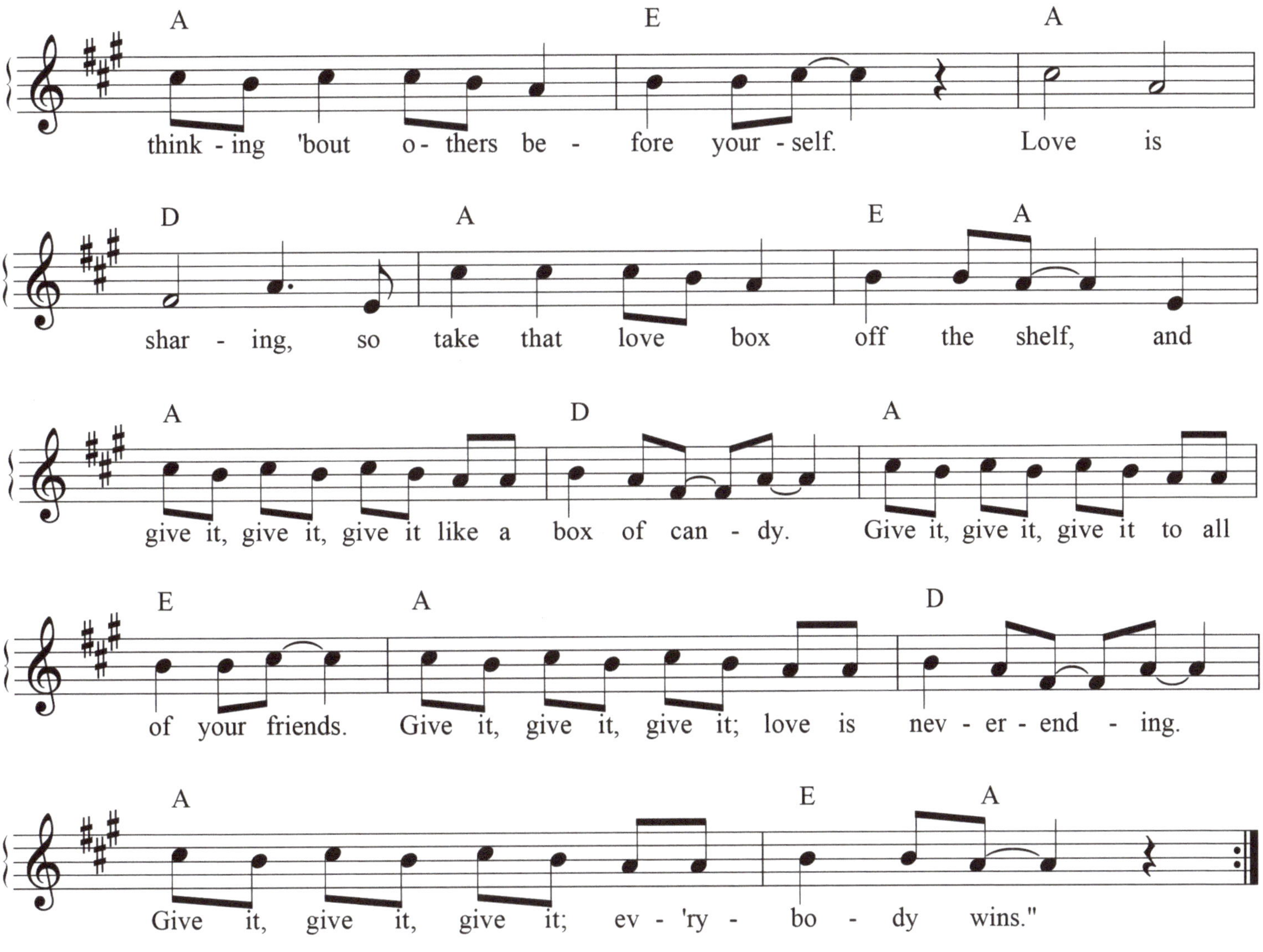
A E A
think - ing 'bout o - thers be - fore your - self. Love is
D A E A
shar - ing, so take that love box off the shelf, and
A D A
give it, give it, give it like a box of can - dy. Give it, give it, give it to all
E A D
of your friends. Give it, give it, give it; love is nev - er - end - ing.
A E A
Give it, give it, give it; ev - 'ry - bo - dy wins."

Flower Child

Chords by Alicia Motter-Vlahakos

Words & Music by Cynthia Butler

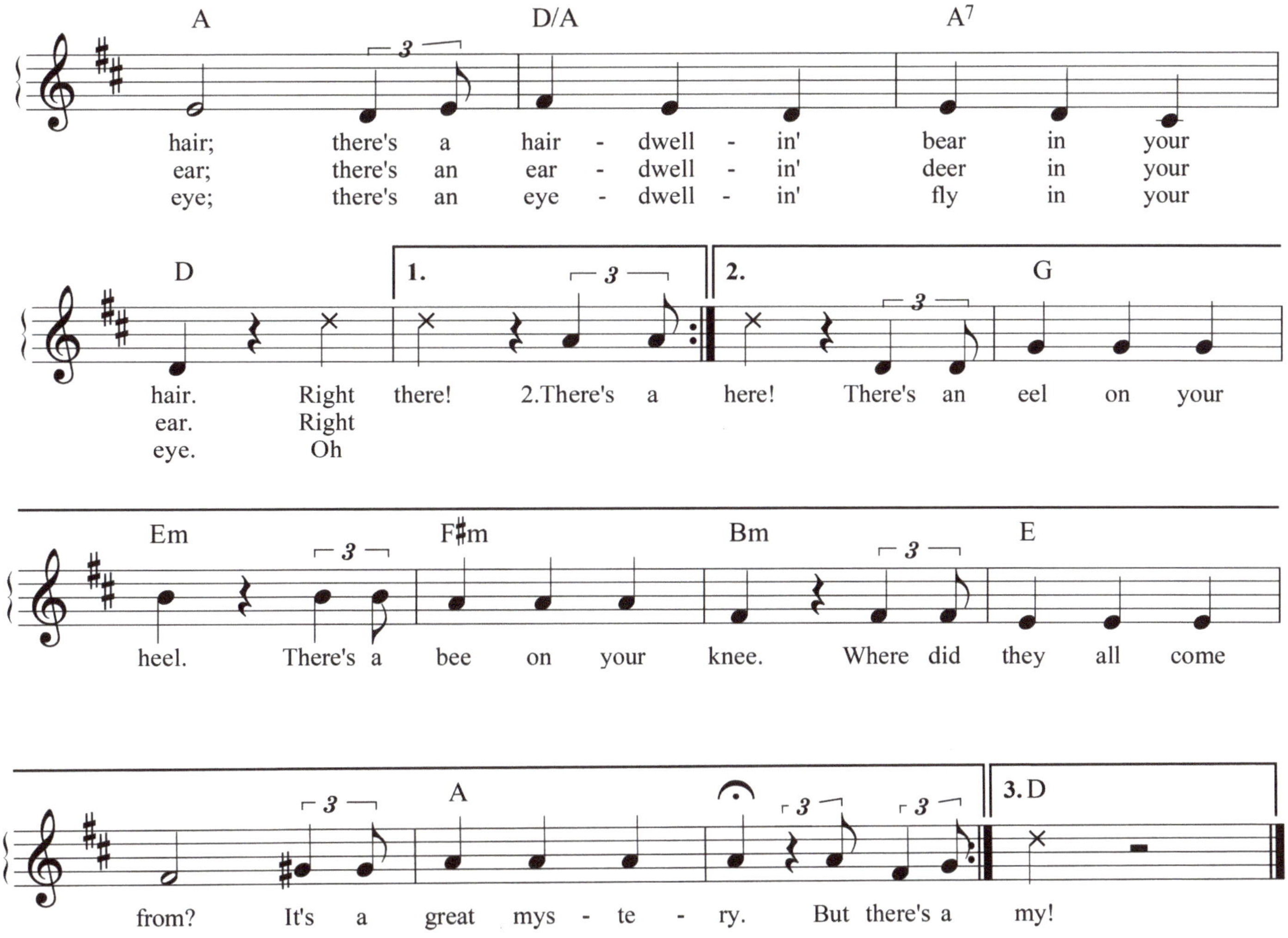
A
D/A
A7
hair; there's a hair - dwell - in' bear in your
ear; there's an ear - dwell - in' deer in your
eye; there's an eye - dwell - in' fly in your
D
1.
2.
G
hair. Right there! 2.There's a here! There's an eel on your
ear. Right
eye. Oh
Em
F♯m
Bm
E
heel. There's a bee on your knee. Where did they all come
A
3. D
from? It's a great mys - te - ry. But there's a my!

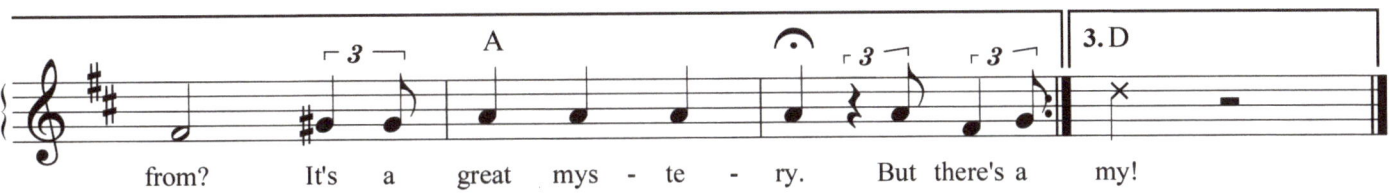

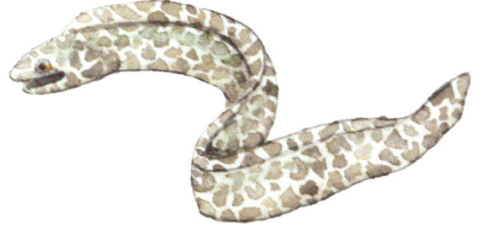

When You Have a Bath

Words & Music by Cynthia Butler

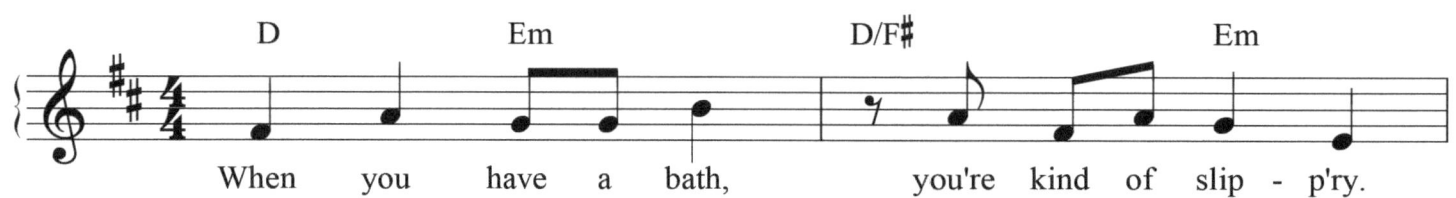
When you have a bath, you're kind of slip - p'ry.

When you have a bath, we wash your bod - y.

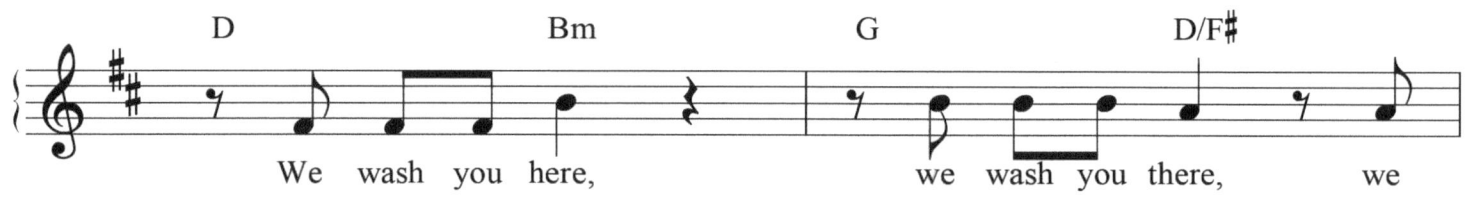
We wash you here, we wash you there, we

wash you from your hair to your lit - tle der - ri - ère.

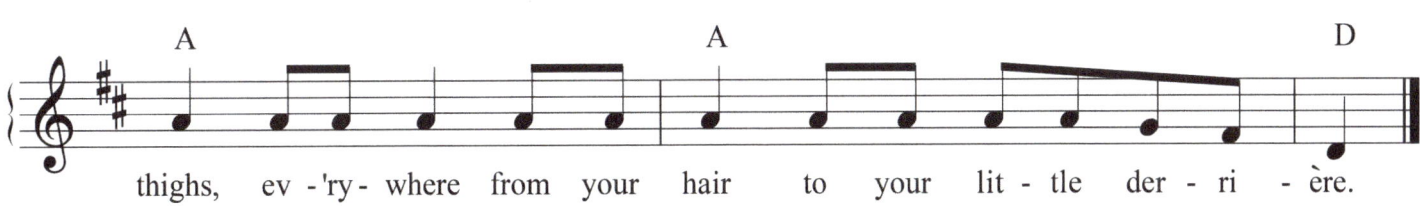

Hippopotamus

Shuffle

Words & Music by Cynthia Butler

The hip - po - pot - a - mus: we like him a lot - a - mus, and we're just

mad - a - pus a - bout the plat - y - pus. We're all quite a - ware of the

po - lar bear, and the el - e - phant is an es - sen - tial el - e - ment. But of all the

an - i - mals, you're just out - stand - i - mal. I would trade a whole zoo for

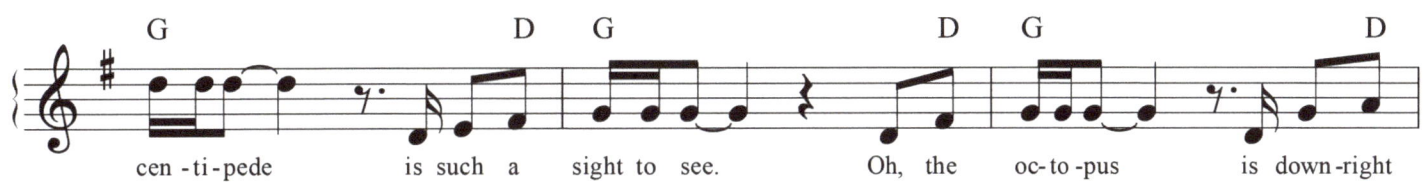

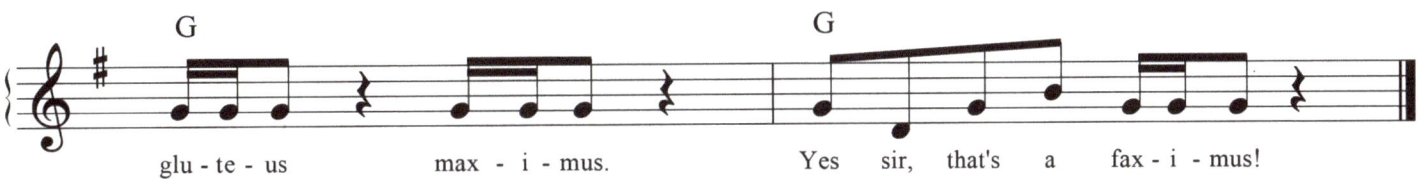

Sleep, Little Caterpillar

Words & Music by Cynthia Butler

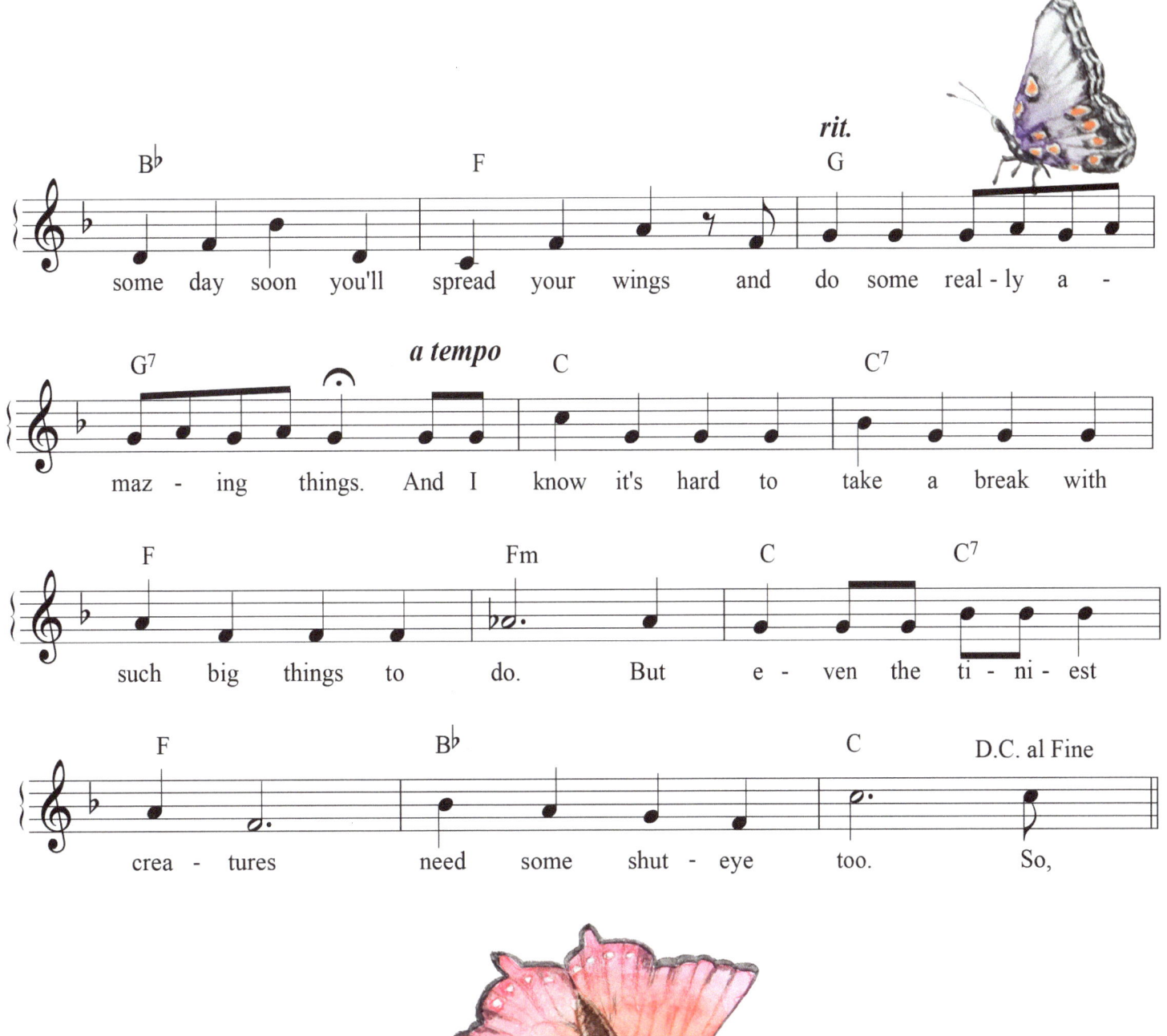

Dreams Take Flight

Words & Music by Cynthia Butler
& Alicia Motter-Vlahakos

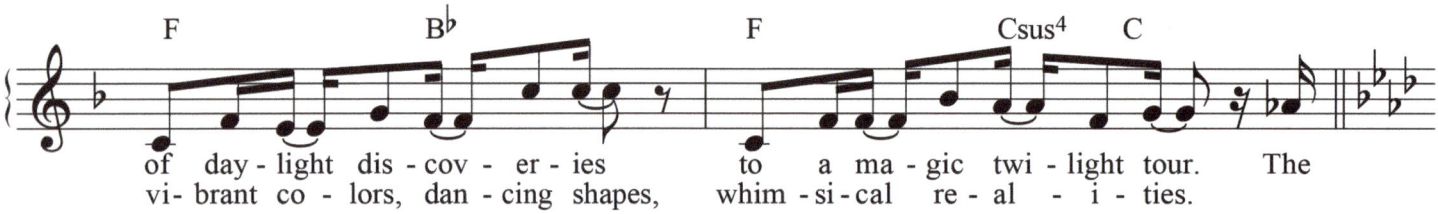

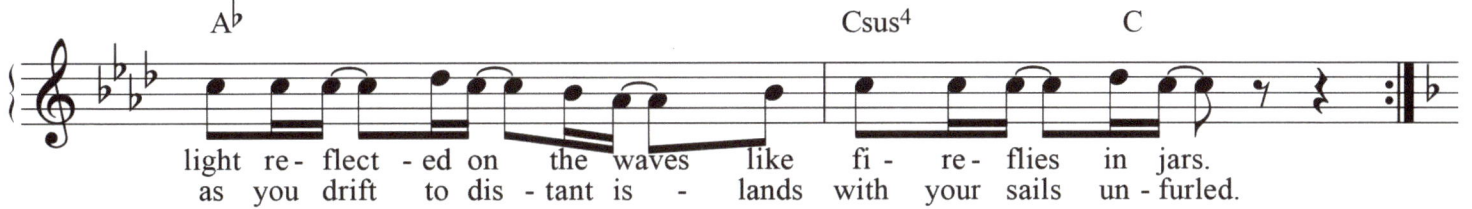

When Kevin and Cynthia Butler were newlyweds of 9 years, Cynthia gave birth to Maranatha Melody. Many other melodies followed as Cynthia wrote little songs to accompany everyday activities with Maranatha. 8 years later this collection of music has grown into a book and recording while the Butlers' baby is growing into a lovely young lady. The family lives in Jewett, TX where Kevin leads worship at First Baptist Church and Cynthia homeschools Maranatha. Kevin contributed his songwriting and editing expertise to this project and Maranatha's 2-year-old voice is featured in "Let's get dressed".

Buddy and Alicia Motter-Vlahakos reside in Clear Lake, TX among palm trees and astronauts. There they teach music lessons at their studio Nassau Bay Music Lessons, perform in various venues and most importantly, raise their precious daughter Séraphine. Alicia contributed her songwriting creativity, vocal prowess, and recording skills to this project. Buddy put the "cherry on the top" by adding a menagerie of instruments, recording effects, and of course the faux-British "Hippopotamus" speech. Buddy and Alicia, along with Kevin and Cynthia, make up the musical group Canopy, pairing their love of music with their heart for Christian ministry.

Kayla Lewis, a woman of many talents, used her skills with graphic design and photography to help bring Cynthia's vision to life. When not pursuing creative interests, Kayla, along with her husband Josh, spend many nights at Cynthia and Kevin's house terraforming Mars, curing the world of pandemics, and having many other board-gaming adventures. Their son Braddock and Maranatha have also had their fair share of adventures running around the living room, jumping on furniture, and singing at the top of their lungs.

Special thanks to flautist Michelle Commons and fiddler Greg Henkel for their musical contributions.

www.ingramcontent.com/pod-product-compliance
Lightning Source LLC
Chambersburg PA
CBHW041118070526
44584CB00002B/205